Getting To Know...

Nature's Children

WOLVES

Judy Ross

PUBLISHER	Joseph R. DeVarennes
PUBLICATION DIRECTOR	Kenneth H. Pearson
MANAGING EDITOR	Valerie Wyatt
SERIES ADVISOR	Merebeth Switzer
SERIES CONSULTANT	Michael Singleton
CONSULTANTS	Ross James
	Kay McKeever
	Dr. Audrey N. Tomera
ADVISORS	Roger Aubin
	Robert Furlonger
	Gaston Lavoie
EDITORIAL SUPERVISOR	Jocelyn Smyth
PRODUCTION MANAGER	Ernest Homewood
PRODUCTION ASSISTANTS	Penelope Moir
	Brock Piper

EDITORS

Katherine Farris	Anne Minguet-Patocka
Sandra Gulland	Sarah Reid
Cristel Kleitsch	Cathy Ripley
Elizabeth MacLeod	Eleanor Tourtel
Pamela Martin	Karin Velcheff

PHOTO EDITORS	Bill Ivy
	Don Markle
DESIGN	Annette Tatchell
CARTOGRAPHER	Jane Davie
PUBLICATION ADMINISTRATION	Kathy Kishimoto
	Monique Lemonnier

ARTISTS

Marianne Collins	Greg Ruhl
Pat Ivy	Mary Theberge

This series is approved and recommended by the Federation of Ontario Naturalists.

Canadian Cataloguing in Publication Data

Ross, Judy, 1942-
  Wolves

(Getting to know—nature's children)
Includes index.
ISBN 0-7172-1941-0

1. Wolves—Juvenile literature.
I. Title.   II. Series.

QL737.C22R67 1985   j599.74'442   C85-098744-X

Have you ever wondered . . .

When you think of a wolf, what comes into your mind? The nasty wolf who dressed up like a grandma to fool Little Red Riding Hood? The big bad wolf who frightened the Three Little Pigs and blew their house down?

In many fairy tales and cartoons wolves are sly and sneaky or just plain mean. No wonder people fear and dislike them.

You might be surprised to learn that, like most wild animals, wolves are probably more frightened of us than we are of them. In addition, wolves are beautiful, intelligent animals who are loyal to each other, live together in families and take special care of their young.

Roly-Poly Pup

With its soft, fuzzy coat and baby-blue eyes a wolf pup looks a lot like a pet puppy dog.

And, like a puppy dog, a wolf pup loves to play with its brothers and sisters.

As the pups tumble over each other, an adult wolf stands guard nearby. If this "babysitter" senses danger, it will quickly send the pups scurrying into the safety of their den.

Play teaches the wolf pup many things. Perhaps the most important lesson is its place in their family, or "pack." When a pup begins to lose in a play fight, it rolls over on its back, ending the fight. The stronger pup is almost always the winner. It stands with its tail in the air, as if to say, "I am the ruler here!" This is the law of the pack—the weaker always obeys the stronger.

Before this pup's first birthday it will be almost as large as its parents.

Dog Cousins

Wolves are related to coyotes, foxes, jackals, dingos and to our pet dogs.

People often get the wolf and its cousin, the coyote, mixed up because they look so much alike. But if you could put a wolf and a coyote side by side, you would see that wolves are larger and stockier than coyotes.

This is a Timber Wolf—the most common kind of wolf. It is the largest wild member of the dog family.

Fox

Coyote

Wolf

Timber Wolf.

Where They Live

Wolves used to live all over North America, but today their range is much smaller. They live mostly in the wilderness parts of Canada and in Alaska. Some wolves prefer to live in forested areas, while others live farther north in the tundra where there are no trees. The forest-dwellers are usually gray to black in color; the tundra-dwellers are generally lighter in color.

Our North American wolves have relatives in Asia, Italy, Scandinavia and parts of Eastern Europe.

The Wolf Up Close

You have heard of the Big Bad Wolf, but how big are wolves in real life? Some large males weigh over 45 kilograms (100 pounds) and are two metres (6 feet) from nose to tail tip. But most males are about the size of a German Shepherd and the females are considerably smaller.

Although some wolves look a lot like German Shepherds, they have longer legs and bigger feet than these dog relatives. And their bodies look more streamlined because their chests are narrower.

Wolves come in a wide range of colors. Some are black, others are white and still others are any color in between. Sometimes wolf pups in the same litter will even have different colors of coats.

Wolf tracks.

On the Move

Like dogs, wolves run on their toes. This lets them take longer strides. For a short distance they can run about 45 kilometres (24 miles) an hour. Although that is pretty fast, most of the animals wolves hunt for food are even faster and those that are not can often escape by zigzagging and turning suddenly. But wolves have one advantage. They are almost tireless and can run for hours.

Most wolves are also amazingly strong and agile. A full-grown wolf can leap as high as a one-storey building.

Long distance runner!

A Big Family

You will not often see a wolf on its own.
Wolves like company and live in family groups
called packs. The members of the pack are
usually the mother and father and their young,
along with aunts, uncles and cousins. Most
wolf packs have seven or eight members, but
some have as many as 14.

The pack always has a leader—the strongest
male in the group. Every other pack member
knows its place and quickly learns to "follow
the leader."

Wolf families are affectionate and co-
operative. They play and hunt together. They
protect each other too. If one wolf gets into
trouble, the others will try to help it.

Leader of the Pack

It is easy to tell which wolf is the pack leader. He is usually the biggest. He stands proud and tall with his tail and head held high. He is the king and he knows it. When he approaches another wolf in his pack, it will cower and skulk, hang its head down and put its tail between its legs. Then it will roll over on its back as if to say, "I give up—you are too strong for me!" This is why wolves seldom fight among themselves. The weaker ones almost always give in before a real fight begins.

Occasionally a wolf does live alone. No one knows for sure why this happens, but it is a hard life without the safety of the pack. Lone wolves often die.

The pack leader often displays his authority by staring at his fellow pack members. The submissive wolves will usually turn away.

Always Alert

Although wolves lie about relaxing in the sun, they are always alert, looking for their next meal or watching for danger.

Luckily wolves have super senses to help them. Like a dog, a wolf has good hearing and can hear high-pitched sounds that people cannot hear. If another pack of wolves is howling many miles away a wolf will hear every howl and know where they are coming from. To do this, it swivels its ears around until it has found the source of the sound.

The wolf also has an acute sense of smell to help it sniff out prey and good eyesight to catch any nearby movement that may signal danger or food.

The wolf has very keen hearing and can detect sounds up to 10 kilometres (6 miles) away.

Wolf Talk

When you talk to your friends you say words out loud. But wolves can "talk" to each other without making a sound. When a wolf's ears point straight up and its teeth are bared, it is warning others to "watch out!" When the pupils of its eyes become narrow slits and its ears are flattened against its head, it is saying, "What's going on here?"

"I'm in charge."

The wolf uses its tail to send messages too. A tail held high tells other wolves, "I'm in charge here." When a wolf tucks its tail between its legs, it is saying, "I'm not going to argue!"

It is easy to tell when a wolf is happy. Like a dog, it tilts its head and wiggles its body from side to side.

"You're the boss."

All members of the wolf pack recognize these different messages. But when they want to have a long-distance conversation with another pack there is nothing like a good howl for keeping in touch.

Opposite page:

Wolves usually spend hot summer afternoons resting.

A Howling Good Time

Wolves seem to really enjoy howling. Sometimes they howl to gather their pack together before a hunt or to let another wolf pack know they are nearby. But at other times they gather close to each other, wag their tails and seem to howl just for the fun of it.

Some people say that once you have heard a wolf howling you will never forget the sound. The range of a wolf's voice is similar to ours. When several howl together, they sound like an eerie choir.

Some people have learned to imitate a wolf's howl and sometimes wolves will answer back. Perhaps they cannot tell the difference!

Besides howling, wolves make other sounds too. They bark, yelp, whine and snarl—just like a dog.

Wolves do most of their howling at night, but they may well decide to call during the day too.

No Trespassing!

Home for the wolf pack may be a huge area, anywhere from 160 to 400 square kilometres (100-250 square miles). The pack will hunt in this territory and defend it against any wolves from other packs. Occasionally, however, packs do join together for winter hunting.

The wolf pack follows the same hunting routes over and over again, trotting along logging roads or the bank of a river, constantly on the lookout for their next meal.

Some days the pack may travel as many as 95 kilometres (60 miles) without finding anything to eat. All along the route they mark the territory by spraying urine on the trees and shrubs. These scent markings are a sign to other wolves that, "This territory is taken—so keep out!"

Team Hunters

Wolves are carnivores, which means that they eat mainly meat. They often hunt alone to catch the small animals and birds that make up much of their diet. But usually the members of the pack will join together to hunt a large animal, such as a caribou, elk or moose.

When this happens, the wolves work together as a team. Sometimes the wolves trick their prey. They divide into two groups and set up an ambush. One group will drive the prey animal toward the rest of the pack which is lying in wait. But even though wolves are clever hunters, most of their prey escape and sometimes the pack goes for days without food.

In the Arctic the Timber Wolf's coat is often pure white.

Hungry as a Wolf

Can you imagine eating a big turkey all by yourself? A full-grown wolf can eat as much as nine kilograms (20 pounds) of meat at one time. That is about the amount of meat on a really big turkey.

Good manners are important when a pack has made a large kill. The leader of the pack always eats first and chooses the best pieces of meat. Next the other members of the pack eat one after the other. Anyone who tries to butt in is met with snarls and barks. The message is clear: "Wait your turn."

Sometimes food that is not eaten is buried or hidden in a hollow log so that the wolves can return for it later. If there are no leftovers and hunting is bad, a wolf can live for several weeks without food. Sometimes the weakest members of the pack get nothing to eat for even longer than that.

Like all of us, a wolf enjoys a cool drink.

Cold Weather Survivors

If a wolf lives where winters are long and cold, it will grow a thick two-layered coat to keep it warm. Long, coarse guard hairs shed rain and snow, while the thick, short underfur traps body-warmed air next to the wolf's skin.

The treads on your snowboots keep you from slipping on icy roads in winter. The wolf has similar treads on its feet—strong tufts of hair that grow between the cushiony foot pads. These help grip the ice when the wolf is traveling across frozen lakes.

Since the wolf is so well equipped to run on ice, a deep snowfall with an icy crust on top makes hunting big game easier for it. The wolf is light enough to run on top of the snow without breaking through the crust, but the larger animal it is chasing sinks through into the deep snow and then cannot escape.

Well dressed for winter.

Loyal Mates and Good Parents

Toward the end of winter the male and female wolf mate. In a pack it is usually only the strongest pair who become parents. If all of the wolves mated, the pack would become too big.

Naturalists believe that wolves pair for life. Both mother and father look after the young and are very good, caring parents. If the mother dies, the father will try to take care of the pups on his own. If he cannot, another adult in the pack will adopt the babies and care for them as if they were its own.

A Cozy Den

Before the pups are born, the mother wolf searches for a birth den. She looks for an underground den, perhaps one that has already been used by a fox or badger. If she cannot find a ready-made den, she will dig one of her own, usually in the side of a sandy hill.

Digging the den is hard work for the mother wolf. First she digs a tunnel that is as long as a car. This tunnel slopes up so that rain will not run into it and it is narrow so that bigger animals cannot crawl into it. At the end of the tunnel, she hollows out a room just big enough for her and her litter.

Once she has her den ready, the mother wolf can relax and rest while awaiting the arrival of her pups.

Spring Pups

The wolf pups are born in the spring. Sometimes there are as many as fourteen of them in the litter, but usually only six or seven.

The newborn pups are very tiny at birth. They weigh about as much as a loaf of bread. They have fine woolly hair that is a sooty blue-gray color and their eyes are shut. They are helpless, so the mother wolf keeps them well hidden in the den. She protects them and lets them snuggle in her warm fur and drink her milk.

For the first two weeks even the father stays away so that the mother wolf and her babies are left undisturbed. Then he begins to visit, usually bringing food for the mother. He is greeted by the excited pups who now stagger about on wobbly legs with their eyes open.

By this time they are growing thicker fur coats.

Wolf families are very affectionate.

Happy Relatives

The birth of the pups is a big event for the pack. For several weeks the pups' aunts and uncles gather around the entrance to the den. When the month-old pups make their first appearance outdoors, the whole pack takes turns playing with them. It is as if they are celebrating the pups' arrival.

You might not even guess that the pups are brothers and sisters because they all look so different. Some pups are pure black, others are speckled beige and still others are somewhere in between. Wolves seem to love babies. They are affectionate and caring with the new pups. They guard them carefully from predators such as eagles or wolverines and keep them from accidentally running into porcupines. When the mother goes off to hunt, an aunt or uncle stays behind to "pupsit."

After three months, wolf pups no longer sleep in their den.

Many Mouths to Feed

As the pups get bigger the birth den becomes cramped and stuffy. So the mother moves her new family to a bigger den. On moving day she carries one pup at a time in her mouth, gently gripping them by the loose skin on their necks.

By age two months, the pups are ready to eat meat. All the family members help to feed them. They bring back meat from the kill in their stomachs. When the pups lick the adult's jaws, the adults bring the food back into their mouths. They then give this half-digested food to the pups.

This may not sound very appealing to you, but it makes a lot of sense for the wolf. If it had to carry fresh meat back to the den a trail would be left leading right to the helpless pups. By carrying the food home in its stomach the wolf keeps the location of the den a secret from other predators. Also, it is much easier for wolves to carry food in their stomachs for long distances.

Opposite page:

Like many young animals, wolf pups are very curious.

Living and Learning

There is much for a wolf pup to learn before it can become an active member of the pack.

The most important lesson is learning its place in the pack. By playfighting and wrestling the pups learn who is strongest and therefore who is dominant.

The next important lesson is how to hunt. The pups pounce on twigs and leaves—and sometimes on each other! These playful games teach them how to stalk prey and set up ambushes.

This pup still has lots to learn!

Joining the Hunt

By the fall the pups look like smaller versions of their parents. They are getting better at hunting games. They practice chasing and catching small animals like mice and frogs.

They have also learned to obey their elders. If they forget their manners they get a gentle smack from one of the adults. By the time their first winter comes, the pups are ready to join in when the pack hunts.

Leaving Home

A winter of hunting with the pack polishes the young wolves' hunting skill. By spring they are skilled hunters. If their pack is small the young wolves may stay with their parents. But if their pack is too large, they will leave. Some will join with other young wolves and start a new pack of their own. Others will become part of another established pack. In the safety of the pack the wolves may live to be 10 or more years old.

Special Words

Carnivore   Animal that eats mainly meat.

Den   Animal home.

Guard hairs   Long coarse hairs that make up the outer layer of the wolf's coat.

Litter   The name for the young in one family.

Mate   To come together to produce young.

Pack   A group of as many as 14 wolves, usually related, that live together.

Predator   An animal that hunts other animals for food.

Prey   An animal hunted by another animal for food.

Pup   The name for a young wolf.

Territory   Area that an animal or group of animals lives in and often defends from other animals of the same kind.

Tundra   Flat land in the Arctic where no trees grow.

INDEX

Cover Photo: Stephen J. Krasemann (Valan Photos)

Photo Credits: Stephen J. Krasemann (Valan Photos), pages 4, 8, 12; J.D. Markou (Miller Services), pages 7, 29; Norman Lightfoot (Eco-Art Productions), pages 15, 16, 20; Wayne Lynch (Master File), page 19; Bob Hyland (Valan Photos), pages 23, 43; J.D. Taylor (Miller Services), pages 24, 26; Tim Fitzharris (First Light Associated Photographers), pages 30, 36; Dennis Schmidt (Valan Photos), page 33; Esther Schmidt (Valan Photos), page 34; J.D. Markou (Valan Photos), pages 40, 45.

Getting To Know...

Nature's Children

WHALES

Mark Shawver

PUBLISHER	Joseph R. DeVarennes
PUBLICATION DIRECTOR	Kenneth H. Pearson
MANAGING EDITOR	Valerie Wyatt
SERIES ADVISOR	Merebeth Switzer
SERIES CONSULTANT	Michael Singleton
CONSULTANTS	Ross James
	Kay McKeever
	Dr. Audrey N. Tomera
ADVISORS	Roger Aubin
	Robert Furlonger
	Gaston Lavoie
EDITORIAL SUPERVISOR	Jocelyn Smyth
PRODUCTION MANAGER	Ernest Homewood
PRODUCTION ASSISTANTS	Penelope Moir
	Brock Piper

EDITORS

Katherine Farris	Anne Minguet-Patocka
Sandra Gulland	Sarah Reid
Cristel Kleitsch	Cathy Ripley
Elizabeth MacLeod	Eleanor Tourtel
Pamela Martin	Karin Velcheff

PHOTO EDITORS	Bill Ivy
	Don Markle
DESIGN	Annette Tatchell
CARTOGRAPHER	Jane Davie
PUBLICATION ADMINISTRATION	Kathy Kishimoto
	Monique Lemonnier

ARTISTS

Marianne Collins	Greg Ruhl
Pat Ivy	Mary Theberge

This series is approved and recommended by the Federation of Ontario Naturalists.

Canadian Cataloguing in Publication Data

Shawver, Mark.
 Whales

(Getting to know—nature's children)
Includes index.
ISBN 0-7172-1897-X

1. Whales—Juvenile literature.
I. Title. II. Series.

QL737.C4S5 1984   j599.5   C84-099568-7

Have you ever wondered . . .

What animal is bigger than any other animal on Earth, but has no teeth? If you guessed the Blue Whale, congratulations! The mighty Blue can grow to weigh as much as 21 African elephants. That is bigger than any dinosaur ever was.

Have you ever heard someone talking about having "a whale of a time"? That usually means that the person had a lot of fun, or a lot of trouble, or a lot of something-or-other. When you think of a whale, you think of something big, so it is not surprising that people sometimes use the word whale when they mean a LOT of something.

Yet not all whales are big. Did you know that some whales, such as the dolphin and the porpoise, are no bigger than a person? There are probably a lot of things about whales that will surprise you.

Long-distance traveler. (Gray Whale)

Not a Big Fish

Are whales big fish? No! There is one very big difference between fish and whales; whales are mammals, just like dogs, or cats or even you.

Because whales live in the sea, they are called marine mammals.

Mammals are animals that have lungs and breathe air. Just as you must swim up to the surface for a gulp of air after an underwater dive, so too do whales. They swim up to the surface from time to time and take in air through a blowhole. Fish do not need to do this. Instead they take the oxygen they need

Lungs extract oxygen from air taken in through blowhole.

Whiskers at some stage in life.

Young born alive.

Horizontal tail fin moves up and down.

WHALE

right from the water through their gills.

Mammals are warm blooded. That means that no matter how cold it is, their body temperature stays much the same. And mammals, including whales, are born alive and take milk from their mother.

Finally, all mammals have hair, at least during one stage of their life. With marine mammals, the hair appears only as whiskers. All whales are born with whiskers, and some keep them all their lives. With most whales, however, the whiskers fall off a few days after they are born.

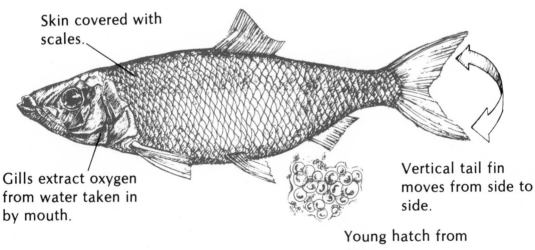

Skin covered with scales.

Gills extract oxygen from water taken in by mouth.

Vertical tail fin moves from side to side.

Young hatch from eggs.

FISH

Once Upon a Time, Long Ago . . .

Scientists believe that some 70 million years ago whales lived on land and looked very different. Why did they become water animals?

Perhaps food ran out on land, and the hungry whales went into the sea looking for food. Perhaps they stayed in the water to keep away from land enemies. Little by little, over many many generations, their bodies changed so that living in the sea would be easier. For instance, whales now have flippers instead of hands and feet like yours. But a whale's flippers have bones very much like those found in human hands. It seems likely that when whales lived on land, they had hands. As time passed, their hands slowly became flippers so that they could swim better. This is just one of many changes the land whales may have gone through to become sea whales.

Whales were probably smaller when they lived on land. Only animals living in water can grow as big as some whales do because the water supports their body weight.

A Whale of a Family

Whales are not only big in size, they also belong to a big family. There are over ninety different kinds of whales—from the small porpoise to the giant Blue Whale.

There are two main types of whales in this whale of a family: whales with teeth and whales without teeth. These two types of whales eat different foods and catch their food in different ways. They are also different in size. In general, the big whales are toothless whales. As well, a male toothed whale is larger than a female, but in the toothless group, the female is usually bigger than the male.

Overleaf:

The Finback Whale is named for its large dorsal fin.

Human Hand   Whale flipper.

Notice the similarity between the bones in the whale's flipper and those in a human hand.

Whales with Teeth

Toothed whales can be small like the dolphin and porpoise, or quite big, like the Sperm Whale.

Small or big, however, toothed whales are dainty eaters—they eat one fish at a time, swallowing it whole. They use their teeth for catching hold of their food, not chewing it.

Toothed whales eat mostly small fish and squid. Some use suction to suck food up from the ocean floor, much as a vacuum cleaner sucks up dirt and crumbs. Most often, toothed whales are seen traveling and hunting in groups called schools or herds. Sometimes hundreds of whales travel together in one herd and they work together to corral or trap fast-moving fish. When fishermen see these herds of whales, they know that lots of fish must be nearby.

Some toothed whales have more than 200 teeth, but the Narwhal (sometimes called the Unicorn Whale) usually has only one.

The Toothless Whales

The whales without teeth are called baleen whales. Instead of teeth, they have as many as 400 plates called baleen hanging down from the roof of their mouth. They use the baleen to filter food out of the water. How?

Baleen whales are gulpers. They swim with their mouths open taking in tonnes of water full of plankton and tiny fish. Then, they close their mouths and drain the water back out through the baleen. The plankton and fish cannot get through and are trapped in the baleen. Then the whale's mighty tongue scoops up the food and the whale swallows it.

Baleen whales are called the great whales because they are so big. Even the smallest of the great whales, the Minke, is about as long as two cars! Would you have guessed that animals that eat such tiny bits of food could grow to be the biggest animals on Earth? Of course, they eat huge amounts. A Blue Whale may well eat 4000 kilograms (9000 pounds) in one day.

Opposite page:

Despite their large size whales are very streamlined and move through the water with ease.

14

The Better Not to See You

If you could look down at a whale in the water, the dark color on its back would blend in with the darker water below. If you were underwater and a whale swam above you, its light underside would blend in with the light from above. This type of coloring—dark top and light underside—is called counter-shading. It makes it harder for the whale's enemies and prey to see it in the water.

Baleen whales' bodies are usually light gray to brown or black on top with a lighter underside. Toothed whales range in color from the pure white Beluga Whale to the coal black Pilot Whale, but most of them, too, are gray with a lighter underside.

Since the Beluga is the only pure white whale in the world it is often called the White Whale. In fact, Beluga means "white one" in Russian.

Coming Up for Air

A whale cannot breathe through its mouth as you can. It gets air by breathing through an opening on the top of its head called a blowhole. This blowhole acts like a kind of nose. And because it is at the top of its head, a whale can breathe without having to stick its whole head out of the water.

As the whale's head comes to the surface of the water and into the air, the nostrils in its blowhole open and let out the used air in a "cough." The whooshing sound of the air being let out can be heard a long way away. Then new air is taken in, the nostrils shut and the whale's head slides under the water surface again. Each breath takes only one or two seconds.

A whale would drown if it did not come to the surface for air from time to time. Because of this, whales are not able to sleep for long periods of time. Instead they take short "cat naps" many times a day.

Spotting a Spout

When a whale lets its breath out through its blowhole, you can see it—it looks like a spout of water spray.

It is hard to get close to a whale, but you can often tell one type from another by its spout. The Gray Whale has a short bushy spout. The Sperm Whale shoots out its air on an angle. The Blue Whale has a tall skinny spout. And the Right Whale's spout is shaped like a heart!

A whale's spout is not composed of water as you might think. It is air that becomes visible when the water vapor in it condenses—just as your breath does on a cold day.

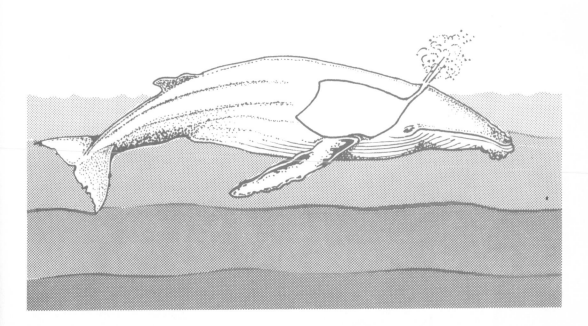

Sights and Sounds

What is it like when you open your eyes underwater? Does everything look blurry? For a whale, it is just the opposite. Whales can see very well under the water, but above the surface, in air, they cannot see well at all!

However, even under water, whales cannot see far; it is often too dark and murky. Whales therefore depend a lot on their keen sense of hearing. Sound travels faster in water than in air, so whales can hear sounds quickly and often from a long way off.

Toothed whales can even "see" with sound. They make a clicking noise that sounds rather like a rusty door being opened and closed. Then they wait for the echo of these clicks to bounce off an object and come back. The time between sending and receiving the clicks tells the whale how far away an object is. The whale can also tell the object's size, shape and the direction in which it is moving.

This process is called echolocation. Scientists have shown how it works by placing small rubber cups over a dolphin's eyes so it could not see. Then they sent the dolphin out to swim through a maze of hoops, and it did it perfectly every time!

Coming to Their Senses

Since whales spend so little time in air, they seem to have lost the sense of smell. (It is not possible to smell things under water.) Instead they have a well-developed sense of taste. Whales in oceanariums are so sensitive to tastes that they will refuse food if it has gone slightly bad.

The whale sends out a series of clicking sounds, sometimes as many as 400 per second. When the sounds reach an object they bounce off and echo back. The timing of the returning clicks tells the whale a great deal about the nature and location of the object.

Echolocation

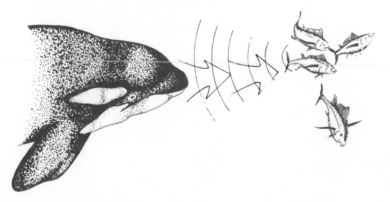

Super Swimmers and Deep Divers

Whales are expert swimmers. They glide through the water by moving their tail fluke up and down. The fluke is very strong, and some whales can swim very fast. The paddle-like pectoral flippers—the "arms" on either side of a whale's body—are sometimes used when turning. The dorsal fin found on the back of most whales helps them to keep steady in the water.

Whales can make long, deep dives into the ocean. To help them do this, they can slow down their heartbeat, so that their air supply lasts longer. During a dive, blood only goes to the most important parts of the whale's body—the brain, heart and lungs. Also, a whale's blood carries more oxygen than that of most other animals.

Toothed whales are good divers because they must often dive deep to catch their food. Baleen whales usually dive down only to about 150 metres (500 feet). They will take a few short, shallow dives, then one long dive that may last for half an hour.

Opposite page:

Notice the barnacles on this Humpback Whale's head. A single whale may have as much as half a tonne of barnacles attached to it!

Nature's Loudest Songs

Whales can make a great variety of sounds including screams, squeaks and moans. But perhaps the whale most famous for its voice is the Humpback.

Humpback Whales are known for their singing. Their songs are among the longest and loudest songs heard in nature. Some may last for 30 minutes and can be heard over a long distance. Scientists are still not sure exactly how whales make these sounds or what they mean. Are they a greeting call? A call for help? Or are they similar to the bark or growl of a dog?

Some people believe the sounds are the way that whales talk to each other. Land animals leave tracks or a scent to send messages to others of their kind. Whales cannot do this, so maybe their underwater sounds are a way to keep in touch with each other.

Humpback Whales.

The Long Journey

A whale may travel thousands of kilometres each year. Some whales roam the oceans freely, but most travel within a certain large area—feeding in one place, mating and giving birth in another. Whales usually feed in cold northern waters and swim to warm southern waters to have their babies. This journey is called migration.

One baleen whale, the Gray Whale, has the longest migration of any mammal in the world. Each year, some of these whales spend summers off the coast of Alaska, then they travel south and spend the winter off the coast of Mexico. Sometimes the journey south will take as long as three months.

Species of whales most commonly found in North American waters (illustration overleaf)

Beluga Whale. A toothed whale that is pure white when fully grown. Found mainly in shallow Arctic waters.

Blue Whale. A baleen whale that weighs about 80,000 kilograms (180,000 pounds). The largest of all whales.

Bottlenose Dolphin. A small toothed whale usually found in warmer waters. The star of most oceanarium shows.

Bowhead Whale. A large baleen whale whose baleen is about 4 metres (14 feet) long, the longest of any whale.

Fin Whale. The fastest swimmer of the baleen whales, going 12 kilometres (20 miles) per hour. Prefers deep waters.

Gray Whale. Fairly large baleen whale that spends a lot of time near shore. In recent years some have become quite friendly.

Humpback Whale. A baleen whale that has very large flippers, up to 5 metres (16 feet) in length. The most active of the baleen whales.

Killer Whale. A toothed whale that grows to about 9 metres (30 feet). It is known for its intelligence—and for its big appetite.

Narwhal A toothed whale, the male of which (and very occasionally the female) has an external tusk that may reach a length of 3 metres (10 feet).

Minke Whale. The smallest of the baleen whales, the Minke seems to eat fish more often than any other baleen whale.

Right Whale. In early whaling days this baleen whale was considered the ''right'' one to hunt because it is such a slow swimmer.

Sperm Whale. The largest of the toothed whales and the deepest diver in the ocean. May dive more than 2 kilometres (3 miles) down.

KILLER WHALES

FIN WHALE

BOWHEAD

BELUGA

GRAY WHALE

BOTTLENOSE DOLPHINS

SPERM WHALE

HUMPBACK

MINKE WHALES

NARWHAL

WHALE

RIGHT WHALE

Blanket of Blubber

Gray Whales and some other kinds of whales spend the summer months in the cold waters of the north because there is lots of food there. The whales eat huge amounts and store some of what they eat as fat in a thick layer of blubber. The Bowhead Whale, for example, has blubber that is more than half a metre (2 feet) thick! This layer of blubber acts like a thick winter coat. It helps to keep a whale warm by keeping in its body heat and keeping out the cold.

In the early winter, when ice begins to form over the water and there is not as much food, the whales begin to swim south. During their journey they do not stop to eat or even to rest.

Some whales, such as the Beluga and Narwhal, stay in the colder waters all year round. In the winter, when food is scarce, they absorb the stored fat in their blubber to give them energy.

Beluga Whale.

All in the Family

Most whales are ready to mate when they are about six years old. Mating whales play together and have been seen jumping and splashing about with each other. They gently nuzzle and "sing" to each other as they press their giant bodies together. Sometimes two males will fight over a female.

Whales are choosy about a mate, and once they have chosen, they are very affectionate. They splash in the water together, roll together and hug each other with their flippers. Some types of whales may even stay together for life.

No one is sure why whales breach, but it may be just for the fun of it!

A Warm Water Cradle

Females usually give birth to one baby, called a calf, every two or three years. Since a baby whale does not have a layer of blubber to keep it warm, it is best if it is born in warm water.

Some whale babies, such as those of the Gray Whale and the Humpback, are born in warm lagoons and shallow inlets. There they are safe from the cold, crashing waves of the ocean and safe from enemies, such as sharks and Killer Whales.

Narwhals and other whales that do not migrate to warmer waters simply move closer to the shore during the arctic summer to have their calves.

A baby whale can keep up with its fast-swimming mom by keeping close to her side. The water passing between their two bodies actually pulls the calf along.

A Big Beautiful Baby

A baby whale is huge! A newborn Blue Whale, for example, may weigh 2000 kilograms (4400 pounds) and be as long as two cars.

Although baby whales are born under water, they do not stay there long. They cannot breathe under water. As soon as her baby is born, the mother quickly helps it get to the surface for its first breath of air. She does this by pushing it up with her snout and guiding it with her flippers. Other female whales may help her.

A newborn whale is a very hungry baby! Just like a human baby, the newborn calf gets milk from its mother. It nuzzles close to her and nurses on her milk. A big baby Blue Whale can drink what would amount to almost 600 cartons of milk in one day! The milk is very rich, and the calf grows quickly.

The baby whale stays close to its mother, swimming under her flippers. A mother whale will do anything to keep her baby from being hurt. If danger is near, a mother whale can become quite fierce.

Opposite page:

Beluga Whales are not born white. It will take about five years before this calf takes on the complete coloring of its parents.

Whale School

One of the first things a mother whale teaches her baby is when to come up for air. The calf learns by imitating its mother's every movement. They swim, surface, breathe and then dive together. Soon the calf has learned what to do, and it is ready to enter the rougher waters of the open ocean.

Unlike a human baby who is completely helpless at birth, a newborn whale is well prepared for life in the ocean. But it still needs the lessons from its mother to improve its skills at surfacing, breathing, swimming and diving.

A baleen calf will nurse from its mother for six to eight months. Calves of toothed whales usually nurse longer—up to two years. They need the longer nursing period because they have more to learn about hunting and catching food than the baleen whales. Toothed whale calves generally stay close to their mother until she becomes pregnant again. After that, the young whale is pretty much on its own, although it will stay with the herd.

A whale of a tail!

There are several places in North America, including the coasts of British Columbia and California, the Gulf of St. Lawrence and the Bay of Fundy, where whales come close enough to shore for people to watch them.

A Whale of a Time

Most whales are playful animals. They spend hours diving and splashing about. They leap high into the air, then come crashing down on their side with a big splash. This is called breaching. Whales seem to enjoy each other and are curious about the world around them.

Many people find it interesting to watch schools of whales in the water. Every year when thousands of Gray Whales migrate to the warm lagoons off the coast of Mexico, whale watchers go out in small boats to look at them. Some of the whales have become very friendly and let the people get close enough to pet them. They may even push a small boat around with their snout or come up under it and lift it gently with their back. All of this is in fun and everyone has a whale of a time! The whales seem to enjoy the whale watchers as much as the whale watchers enjoy them!

Gentle Giants

Whales seem to be very caring animals, and there have been many stories of whales helping each other. Some people once saw two adult Gray Whales helping a baby whale that was stuck on a sandbar. The calf was struggling around on the land and crying out. The two adults jumped out of the water, as if looking for the baby. When they spotted it, they swam over and slid up on the sandbar. With one whale on either side of the baby, they rocked until the calf was tightly sandwiched between them. Then they rocked together until they all slid off the sandbar into the water.

Opposite page:

What lies in the minds of these intelligent animals? No one knows for sure, but scientists hope that someday we will be able to communicate with them.

The Long Trip Back

Many whales stay in the warm breeding waters until spring. Then they are ready to travel to their summer feeding grounds in the north where the food supply is much greater. The new mothers and babies are the last to begin the long journey. This gives the calves extra time to grow and become stronger for the swim north.

Learning about Whales

By studying whales in captivity, scientists have discovered much of what we know about these giants of the sea. But there are still many mysteries about whales for us to uncover.

For thousands of years, people have marveled at the great whales in the sea and wondered how they lived in the wild. Recently, with better underwater equipment, we have been able to study some whales more closely. We know more about whales than we ever have before. Still, the more we learn about them, the more we are fascinated by their intelligence, gentleness and their mastery of their watery world.

Special Words

Baleen   Plates in the upper jaw of some whales that strain out the small animals the whale eats.

Blowhole   Nostril at the top of the whale's head through which it breathes (some whales have two blowholes).

Blubber   A layer of fat under the skin of most marine mammals.

Breaching   The act of a whale leaping out of the water.

Breed   To come together to produce young.

Counter-shading   The coloring of a whale that helps to make it less noticeable.

Fluke   Whale's tail fin.

Echolocation   Method used by some whales to find their way under water by sending out sounds and listening to the returning echoes.

Mammal   Any animal that breathes air, is warm blooded, gives birth to live young, lives on mother's milk when young, and has some kind of hair during some stage of its life.

Migration   To travel from one region or climate to another for feeding or breeding.

Plankton   Small animals and plants that live in the sea.

INDEX

Cover Photo: Bora Merdsoy (Image Index)

Photo Credits: Pat Morrow (First Light Associated Photographers), page 4; Barrett and MacKay (Masterfile), pages 10-11; Janet Foster (Masterfile), page 12; Bora Merdsoy (Image Index), pages 15, 41, 42; Fred Bruemmer, pages 16, 38; R. Galbraith (Valan Photos), pages 19, 27, 45; Esther Schmidt (Valan Photos), page 20; Don Morton (FPG, Miller Services), page 24; T. Gregg Eligh (Miller Services), page 33; Bill Brooks (Master File), page 34; John Foster (Master File), page 37.

All art illustrations: Jenniffer Julich and Jeannette McNaughton